Alpha Male
Become An Alpha Male and Have It All

Women, Relationships, Success, Confidence, and Respect!

By

Alan Anderson

Alan Anderson

© Copyright 2015 by Alan Anderson - All rights reserved.

This document is geared towards providing exact and reliable information in regards to the topic and issue covered. The publication is sold with the idea that the publisher is not required to render accounting, officially permitted, or otherwise, qualified services. If advice is necessary, legal or professional, a practiced individual in the profession should be ordered.

- From a Declaration of Principles which was accepted and approved equally by a Committee of the American Bar Association and a Committee of Publishers and Associations.

In no way is it legal to reproduce, duplicate, or transmit any part of this document in either electronic means or in printed format. Recording of this publication is strictly prohibited and any storage of this document is not allowed unless with written permission from the publisher. All rights reserved.

The information provided herein is stated to be truthful and consistent, in that any liability, in terms of inattention or otherwise, by any usage or abuse of any policies, processes, or directions contained within is the solitary and utter responsibility of the recipient reader. Under no circumstances will any legal responsibility or blame be held against the publisher for any reparation, damages, or monetary loss due to the information herein, either directly or indirectly.

Respective authors own all copyrights not held by the publisher.

The information herein is offered for informational purposes solely, and is universal as so. The presentation of the information is without contract or any type of guarantee assurance.

The trademarks that are used are without any consent, and the publication of the trademark is without permission or backing by

Alan Anderson

the trademark owner. All trademarks and brands within this book are for clarifying purposes only and are the owned by the owners themselves, not affiliated with this document.

Table of Contents

INTRODUCTION..7

CHAPTER 1 – UNDERSTANDING THE ALPHA MALE MINDSET..9
On Top Of the Food Chain...9
Lonely Connotation..10

CHAPTER 2 – IDENTIFYING PROVEN METHODS TO BOOST YOUR CONFIDENCE..13
Talk Your Way..13
Body Language..15

CHAPTER 3 – SPORTING A WINSOME ATTITUDE AT WORK..17
Assuming Your Position...17
Being Attuned To Your Environment..19

CHAPTER 4 – ENSURING SUCCESS IN THE ROMANCE DEPARTMENT...21
Female Predisposition...21

CHAPTER 5 – IMBIBING THE ALPHA MALE PERSONA AS A LIFESTYLE CHOICE...25
Never Enough..25

CHAPTER 6 – WHO IS AN ALPHA MALE? 27
A Roaring Personality..27
Ways to Build A Good Personality..28
Pick Clothes Wisely...28
Building Your Wardrobe..29
Physique...35

CHAPTER 7 – ALPHA MALE AND HIS TONGUE.....................39
What You Speak..40
How You Speak..41
When You Speak..42
No Bullshit Attitude..43

CHAPTER 8 – BASIC FEATURES OF AN ALPHA MALE THAT YOU MUST INCORPORATE INTO YOUR PERSONALITY......47

CHAPTER 9 – MASCULINITY: A CHANGING CONCEPT........57

CONCLUSION..59

Introduction

Thank you for downloading my book, ***"Alpha Male: Become An Alpha Male and Have It All: Women, Relationships, Success, Confidence and Respect!"***

This book contains proven steps and strategies to help you determine what it takes to become an alpha male, what its attendant issues are, and how you can imbibe such a mindset to make yourself stand out from the rest.

There has been much talk about the perks of being an alpha male. The fact that you are reading this book goes to show that you are probably interested in becoming an alpha male yourself. There is nothing wrong with this, of course, except that this concept has been beyond idealized. Nowadays, many people subscribe to the rather false notion that alpha males are born and not made. This could not be farther from the truth.

The fact of the matter is that while it is true that part of being an alpha male is genetic in nature -- such as, say, your facial features or bone structure -- a huge part of it, however, is the product of conscious effort and the desire to be on top of your game. Being an alpha male, in other words, entails hard work, self-awareness, sacrifices, and a consistently strong resolve to continue improving yourself. You just do not sit around, bask in your self-defined awesomeness, and expect everything to fall into place magically. That is certainly not how it works.

On this end, this book serves as a quick guide to help you achieve alpha male status. The succeeding chapters discuss at length the steps you need to undertake to develop the skills and confidence you need to attract the women you want, be on top of your professional career, and earn the respect and admiration of your peers. The road towards achieving these goals is not easy, but with a fair amount of discipline and commitment, there is hardly any reason why you cannot achieve them.

Thanks again for downloading this book. I hope you enjoy it!

Alan Anderson

Chapter 1 – Understanding The Alpha Male Mindset

A key concept in the study of the biological evolution of living things is the "survival of the fittest." This idea presupposes that all things being equal, only those who are strong or fit enough to withstand the challenges and risks to their very survival will have the chance to live longer lives and breed their own kind. The confluence of natural forces leaves little regard for the weak, such that those who cannot protect themselves ultimately face the risk of becoming extinct.

The beauty of this concept is that it is not exclusive to the study of flora and fauna. In fact, when we place it in the context of our day-to-day human experience, it can very well lend an explanation as to the way some individuals manage to succeed at getting what they want and the way some falter. It is a dog-eat-dog world out there, so goes a popular maxim, and only those who are made of sterner stuff are likely to end up successful.

Enter the alpha male. Over the years, a lot has been written about what makes a man an alpha male. Just as much literature has been published on ways to imbibe the traits, characteristics, and elements that all together constitute the modern day incarnate of the alpha male.

However, what exactly does it take to be referred to as an alpha male?

On Top Of the Food Chain

As the name suggests, an alpha male is someone who symbolically sits atop the food chain -- someone who ranks above his peers in terms of physical demeanor, professional undertakings, intellectual pursuits, and romantic exploits, among others. This is a guy to whom everything seems to come easy, and as such, succeeds at everything he does; it is almost unfair.

A number of traits that ultimately make him stand out from everyone else mark the alpha male. Armed with charisma, likeable character, confident demeanor, decisive front, and a go-getter personality, the alpha male knows what he wants, is passionate about what he does, and is committed in achieving his goals. It is no wonder then that the people around him could not help, but admire him.

Conversely, someone who is not an alpha male is referred to as a beta male. The latter is a rather denigrating term used to refer to a man who neither possesses nor exhibits the hallmark traits of the former. As such, a beta male is essentially a nameless and faceless character whose life and professional career are marked by mediocrity, a degree of regularity, and the dismal lack of excitement.

Lonely Connotation

Given its rather lonely connotation, it is hardly surprising that no one wants to be called a beta male. This is precisely the reason why many men desire to imbibe the alpha male mindset, if only to dispel the notion that they are living mediocre lives.

What these men fail to acknowledge, however, is that being an alpha male is not just simply a state that they can magically summon overnight. Instead, it is a mindset or a lifestyle that demands hard work, practice, commitment and consistency from your end. While it is true that part of being an alpha male is genetic in nature -- such as, say, your facial features and bone structure -- the fact is that being an alpha male is also something that can be honed over time.

The succeeding chapters discuss at length the steps that you can undertake to become an alpha male yourself. The hope is that as you go through this book, you will imbibe the skills and traits needed to boost your confidence, develop a fun and charismatic personality, sport a winsome attitude at work, and succeed in the romance department.

Alan Anderson

Chapter 2 – Identifying Proven Methods To Boost Your Confidence

If there is anything that distinguishes an alpha male from the rest of ordinary men out there, it is the fact that the former acts and talks with greater ease and confidence than the latter. This attitude is to be distinguished from swag, which often connotes an exercise in overcompensation to conceal deep-buried insecurities or bravado, which is a mere mindless put-on for bravery.

Confidence in this sense pertains to your ability to deal with other people and do things without any hint of uneasiness, difficulty, or awkwardness. This key trait is useful in establishing a genuine connection with other people and in carrying out your functions well and without a hitch.

Although intangible, confidence is something that is fairly obvious to anyone who feels or observes it. Conversely, the lack of it is just as noticeable, which is the reason why as you aspire to become an alpha male, the one thing you should learn to focus on is how to boost your confidence.

Confidence is a trait that you can manifest in a variety of ways. From the way you talk to the way you present yourself to others, it is necessary to maintain a level of consistency to show that you know what you are doing and that you are on top of the situation. As an alpha male, anything less will not do.

Talk Your Way
Perhaps, the most obvious way that others can gauge if you are confident or not is by the way you talk. First impressions last, and so coming across as an indecisive nervous wreck at first meeting is a situation that may be tough to rectify. Failure to act

on such a negative impression will inevitably result in the loss of your credibility and the reluctance of people to deal with you.

Thankfully, you can use a number of methods to improve your conversational skills. The first and most important of these methods may not necessarily be the most obvious, and that is to be familiar with your audience or the people you are talking to.

Knowing who your audience is allows you to strategize. This is because a communication approach that works for a particular type of audience may not necessarily work for another, causing a problem along the way. However, if you have a fair understanding of whom you will be talking to -- what their age bracket is, what their interests are, and what they do for a living -- you can adjust and reconfigure your approach to come up with a style that is appropriate and effective.

However, knowing whom you will be talking to is only the first step. You should complement this by your ability to speak in a clear and audible fashion. Alpha males are marked by their aptitude to get themselves across in a direct way using the least number of words. You do not want to make beating around the bush a habit because doing so is only going to make you look clueless, and this is of course the last thing you want to happen.

However, while making yourself understood should be one of your major considerations, you also want to make sure that you do not come across as a stiff or rigid character that means business all the time. As such, use humor for effect. Everyone loves someone who can make people smile or burst into fits of laughter.

Laughter brings people closer together. So the more comfortable people are with you, the likelier that they are going to open up to you. In other words, a light mood eases away unnecessary tension and makes it easy for you to push your agenda, should you happen to have one. You can thereafter use other people's willingness to listen to you to your advantage. This is part of building a charismatic persona, a subject discussed in detail in the succeeding chapters.

Body Language

More than words, however, your demeanor and your body language also spell a huge difference on whether or not you are able to communicate with others with confidence. This aspect of communication encompasses a broad range of factors, including, say, the way you grip other people's hands when giving them a handshake to the way you sit or stand.

For starters, maintain eye contact with the people you talk to. Doing so shows that you are paying attention to what others are saying and that you are listening. Be careful, however, when gazing far too long since people may mistake you for being creepy. Switch from one eye to another, or if you are speaking before a group of three or more, look at their foreheads or the bridge between their eyebrows.

Assume your position as an alpha male by observing proper posture. As such, refrain from slouching or sporting a slacker's demeanor. This is no different from how some primates thump their chests and make themselves look taller as a way of asserting their superiority. In your case, though, you do not need to do any of these except perhaps ensure that your overall composure suggests that you are no ordinary individual.

Toward this end, it would do well to greet people with a firm handshake, which implies a character of conviction and strength. In addition, do away with unnecessary gestures. Sport a degree of self-awareness to learn if your gestures are already bordering on the distracting and annoying, and set up adjustments from there.

In sum, being confident is something that you can definitely work on as you endeavor to become an alpha male. This trait requires effort, commitment, dedication, hard work, and consistency so that you imbibe the proper attitude and not seem as if you are merely putting on a show.

Alan Anderson

Chapter 3 – Sporting A Winsome Attitude At Work

One of the settings where you can correctly display your alpha male demeanor is the workplace, and for good reasons. For one, you want to ensure your continued growth in the organization you belong to, and such a goal requires that you rise above everyone else to get promoted or else be in a better position to climb up the ranks. Second, being assured of your position in the workplace lends greater confidence in yourself to perform better. Third, working with your colleagues becomes so much easier when they have faith in your capability to deliver.

As with anything else, the first thing you need to do is to be clear about your goals and objectives. You do not enter a war without an idea of what you are fighting for and in many ways; your day to day life in the workplace is a battle you have to win every single time. Set out your expectations and ideals on what you want to accomplish and when to achieve these goals. Knowing what you want will no doubt help you in formulating a strategic career plan.

Once you have laid out your professional career plan, get down to the basics. The key is to focus on your principal tasks and responsibilities. It becomes relatively easier for you to manage other duties on the side once you master your basic functions. Not only will this allow you to be more efficient, this also serves as a hallmark of your reliability and outstanding work ethic -- things that will definitely play in your favor over time.

Assuming Your Position

In addition, learn to assume your position. As an alpha male, you want everyone to know that you are certain of your skills and confident in the knowledge that you are an asset to the organization. What this essentially means is that you do not skirt away from your tasks and that you are always on top of things.

In this regard, it would do well to practice the things you have learned in Chapter 2 of this book about being confident and charismatic. Speak out your opinions and make intelligent suggestions without being disagreeable or offensive. Be decisive when needed and never play the blame game. This means you should assume responsibility for the consequences of your actions. In other words, assume an active role in helping shape your career. Standing idly by and expecting great things to happen without doing anything is a mindset you should not even think of sporting at all.

Note, however, that when it comes to looking after your growth in the workplace, being an alpha male can be a double-edged sword. As discussed in the preceding chapters, being personable, having a likeable character, and possessing a commanding presence are some of the essential things that you can do to earn the respect and admiration of your peers. However, this is not a hard and fast rule. You will realize that on certain occasions, possessing any of the aforementioned traits is likely to place you at a disadvantageous position. How?

For one, management officials or even human resources personnel may harbor the fear that with you always being in control and always sporting a confident demeanor, you may have the compulsion to act on your own and therefore be a poor team player. Know that in many, if not all, organizations, the ability to sport a cooperative attitude and the aptitude to consolidate the opinions of everyone is integral. In other words, you may have the charm and confidence to make everyone follow your lead, but unless you are willing to bend over and learn to listen to what others have to say, the probability of being bypassed for promotion remains a real risk.

Being Attuned To Your Environment

So what do you need to do in order to overcome this risk? The answer is simple: Be a team player.

You might be wondering: Aren't being an alpha male and being a team player at odds with each other? How can these two seemingly opposite traits be reconciled?

First, it is necessary to keep in mind that being an alpha male does not mean ignoring the opinion of everyone in the room. Know that it takes maturity, class, and a degree of subtlety to pause for a bit and hear out what others have to say. Great conversationalists are great listeners, too. In the same vein, great leaders are great listeners as well. Without a doubt, the capacity to listen is an integral asset that you as an alpha male should always possess.

Attendant to this is your willingness to listen to other people's feedback about you. Whether it's from your colleagues or your superiors, getting any form of feedback is always a great way to gauge how you are doing and what more needs to be done in order for you to do better moving forward.

Aside from being in touch with other people's sentiments, it is just as crucial to set realistic expectations about what others are capable of. We are talking about perfectionism and its most obvious pitfalls. Note that alpha males are famous for having exacting standards in everything they do, but this is different from being a perfectionist. The former pertains to the quest to make the best out of everything while the latter is an exercise in unsustainability that results to nothing more than disappointments and unhealthy relationships. Take note of the difference.

In sum, being successful in the workplace requires a healthy mix of aggressiveness and subtlety -- things that all alpha males are keenly aware of. As an alpha male, you sport a go-getter attitude to achieve your goals while staying attuned to your environment. It would be unwise to subscribe to the notion that by simply acting on your impulses akin to a raging bull, it would be enough to get what you want. An alpha male can obviously do better than this.

Chapter 4 – Ensuring Success In The Romance Department

One of the more interesting studies conducted by biologists and wildlife experts in the past couple of decades has something to do with the dynamics of the relationship between males and females in certain primate groups, such as chimpanzees and gorillas. Scientists have noted that when it comes to their mating preferences, the female members of these species often favor the strongest and the most dominant male in their group.

As such, there exists a struggle among the male members of the group as to who among them is the strongest, and therefore the most worthy of the affection of the female members. This struggle is a complex interplay of intimidation and sometimes of violence, which at its culmination eventually results in the rise of the so-called alpha male. Consequently, this alpha male enjoys the privilege not only of being the top choice of the female members of his group, but also of being the group's de facto leader.

Many people note that such dynamics evident in the male to female relationships among primates is also applicable to human relationships. As the theory goes, women naturally get attracted to men who display strength, confidence, and the natural ability to rise above the rest. Many argue that such a biological predisposition is innate and is rooted in the natural tendency of females to seek a male partner who is virile enough to bear her an offspring, strong enough to protect her from any form of danger, and enterprising enough to provide for her and her child's needs.

Female Predisposition
When it comes to human relationships, the same dynamics observed among some primates is just as evident. Over the past decades, a lot of research has been conducted as a way of

assessing the patterns of human relationships starting from how two individuals meet, establish a connection, and foster a bond until these two people decide to live together and have a family of their own. Almost always, women are naturally inclined to notice men who display a sense of uniqueness and superiority in intellect, resolve, or strength -- traits that can be classified as anything but mediocre.

Whether or not this female predisposition to prefer alpha males over beta males is instinctive and biological in nature is something that can be certainly looked into, although the most integral takeaway from this is the fact that in romance as in everyday life, alpha males enjoy a significant advantage over the rest of the male population. Their natural flair to charm and draw women in may seem like an injustice for many who work so hard, but still fail to earn the affections of the women they love. The good news, however, is that being an alpha male is not an exclusive trait. In fact, it is something that you, too, can have if you put your mind and heart into it.

The key of course lies in understanding the inner workings of the female psyche. It would be naive to assume that women mindlessly get attracted to men just like that. Unlike most regular men whose attraction to women is driven by a short-term goal of dominating or subduing them, most women think far beyond the short term and into the distant horizon. They think of the future, they think of emotional investment, they think of security, they think of having children, and they think of how life will be like when they are old. When you consider all these factors, the inevitable conclusion is that they desire a man who is more than capable of satisfying these needs, hence their attraction to alpha males.

As such, alpha males are in an enviable position where women see them as ideal partners. However, such a position demands that alpha males should be worthy of its privileges so in many ways, it is something that obviously demands a lot.

From the way they go about it, though, it would seem that alpha males have got the whole romance thing mastered already. They make the entire thing look so easy. So how do they do it? Here are a few of their ways:

1. Learn the Art of Flirtation

This is to be distinguished from brash, rowdy, or machismo-laden attempts at catching women's attention. Know that alpha males are not the "Jersey Shore" kind of guys whose notion of romance involves beer bongs, rap music with explicit lyrics, and non-committal sex. It is far from it.

Flirtation in this sense pertains to subtle moves designed to let a woman know that a guy is into her without necessarily letting out the words for it. This may take the form of meaningful glares, interesting jokes, and engaging conversations, among others. Essentially, alpha males merely set out the path and it goes smoothly from there.

2. It Is Not All about You

Sure, you have the looks, the money, the power, and everyone's attention, but nothing makes a woman feel more special than making her the center of your attention. On dates or even on casual encounters, do not commit the blunder of making everything about you. In other words, do not talk too much about yourself or else face the risk of coming across as a vain and insecure little boy trapped in a man's body, desperately seeking for some form of validation. As an alpha male, the last thing you need is validation because, hey, what for?

3. Make Her Feel Special

Be generous with compliments, but refrain from overdoing it. Engage her in a meaningful conversation about herself -- her likes, her work, her favorite music, and her pet peeves. Lend an ear and be mindful of her body language so you can adjust in case you notice a sudden change in demeanor.

4. Most Importantly, Be True To Yourself

In the first place, there is no reason why you should try to act in a way that does not really reflect who you are. You have worked hard to achieve what you have right now, and it seems rather pointless to have to put up false pretenses. You are smart, you are eloquent, you look good and you are a cut above the rest. At the very least, just be yourself.

In romance as in life, alpha males have the best going for them. However, how do you sustain the alpha male status over time? The next chapter discusses that topic.

Chapter 5 – Imbibing The Alpha Male Persona As A Lifestyle Choice

As has been underscored in the previous chapters, achieving alpha male status takes a lot of hard work and effort. This may not seem immediately obvious, given how alpha males make everything look so easy, but don't be fooled. It took time, a lot of trial and errors, patience, motivation, and a degree of consistency for them to enjoy the fruits of their labor.

It is also worthwhile to point out that being an alpha male is not a one-time exercise. This means that no matter how far you have set yourself apart from the rest, there is still always a room for improvement and an opportunity to learn something new. In other words, complacency is a vice that you should dispense and do away with if you seek to maintain your alpha male status.

In pursuing a sense of self-development, you should always try to achieve a healthy and sustainable balance between inward and outward growth. On the one hand, inward growth refers to the development of your skills, intellect, and emotional aptitude. Outward growth, on the other hand, refers to your physical well-being.

Never Enough

Insofar as inward growth is concerned, never get tired of learning. Always be on the lookout for ways to improve your skills and pick up new learnings to expand your knowledge. Enough, as the saying goes, is never enough.

One way of building upon your knowledge is by looking at the people whose skills and achievements you admire. Learn from them. Figure out what their best practices are and integrate these lessons into your own life. Also, you can try to experiment on your own and try to come up with techniques and strategies that can help you better your circumstances.

In achieving outward growth, the key as an alpha male is to always be in tiptop shape. With your responsibilities and functions, not to mention the expectations heaped on you, it is essential to strive to be healthy. Watch your diet. At the same time, try to work out regularly and take some time to make yourself look presentable at all times.

In sum, being an alpha male is both an aspiration and a lifestyle. Everyone wants to be one, but being one requires a shift in perspective and a commitment to new ways of doing things. While becoming one entails hard work and consistency, it is never too late to achieve this longed-for status yourself. In fact, now is as good a time as any to get started on the road to the top of the food chain.

Chapter 6 – Who Is An Alpha Male?

Welcome to the sixth chapter of this book. Before going further into the features, characteristics and expectations of an ideal alpha male, let us first try understanding that is usually considered an alpha male. Surely, having watched movies and read books, you must have had a rough estimate about the prototype. However, there is more to an alpha male than bulging muscles and pub brawls.

A Roaring Personality

What is your notion of a good personality? One which commands respect and gets noticed as soon as the person wearing it walks into the room, yes? You are somewhat right. Personality is a major aspect of an alpha male profile. Personality is that feature of your existence that creates first impressions. Let me pause for a while here and tell you about first impressions. First impressions are generally misleading, no doubt, but they can have a lasting impression on the minds of on-lookers. Forget about impressions, most times first impressions work wonders for you. A clean-shaven guy, well dressed in a suit stands more chances of landing a job than a badly dressed candidate who slumps his way into the interview room.

An alpha male has a good personality. Not everyone is capable of maintaining a healthy personality but it is not a herculean task to build a personality. Beware of the misconception that looks are all there is to a good personality. They matter but not to an extent from where they can single handedly decide the outcome of your personality. The right components of a personality have been discussed in brief points below.

The first aspect of any good personality is looks. When we say 'looks', we do not mean good looks. Again, 'good looks' doesn't imply the traditional meaning associated with the phrase. Of course your looks matter and have a deciding say in the way your personality will be shaped.

Body posture is another part of your personality that you need to pay attention to. Sometimes the wrong posture could prove to be a total turn off in really otherwise potential circumstances. If you maintain your posture right, it says a lot about your intentions because body posture is considered to be a medium of body language. You convey a lot by the way you talk, walk, sit and get up.

A good personality has, besides looks and physical posture, a good command over the art of speaking. First impressions can take you only so far. After that it is time for you to take matters into your own hands, or tongue to be precise. Your language skills must not only be right but also more than just okay. When you seem to express yourself almost accurately, with regards to what you feel or think, it shows claret of thought and an alpha male is expected to possess a crystal clear thought process about what he wants, needs and should do, say and think.

Ways to Build A Good Personality

A good personality takes time to be built. It is not an overnight process but a longer and more tedious procedure or a series of steps. In order to turn yourself into the ultimate alpha male, you must first focus on changing your personality from an 'also ran' to a winner. Yes, I know it is easier said than done but this section of this chapter will help you realize all the ways in which you can slowly but surely walk towards that alluring personality.

Your first impression decides half the impact you leave behind. Let us first work on how you could leave a good first impression.

Pick Clothes Wisely

Half your first impression is dominated by what you wear. Ever since human has learnt to wrap himself in clothes, trends and fashion updates have always been in vogue. With changing times, needs and tastes, fashion revolutionized itself and has always dominated our times and lives. Clothes are an important part of your personality and should never be ignored while preparing yourself to impress. When you dress up well, it shows that you are a well maintained person and do care about what people think of you. More than that, it says that you are a particular person who knows how to take care of his body.

Know the occasion. Naturally, not every piece of cloth that you wear can be worn to all the social and professional occasions that you become a part of. That is because there is a certain order and a specific unspoken rule regarding the occasions and the respective clothes you could wear to them. When violated, it leads to not just obvious social faux pass but also disastrous effects on the impression you leave behind on your peers' minds.

For example, if it is a social gathering organized by your neighbors, you can choose to wear shorts and a nice button-down t-shirt that would imply that you are out on a casual social get together. Not only would such a get up fit in with the occasion aptly, but it would also show that you are aware of the nature of the gathering and came dressed accordingly. Such an impression builds trust among your friend circles.

If the occasion is your office's party, you might be in trouble for wearing a pair of shorts and bandana, topped with a beach hat. It is natural for you to expect professional faces that would have been accompanied by formal attires. You should try to comply with the given occasion before deciding to open your wardrobe, which brings us to our next topic of discussion: the Wardrobe.

Building Your Wardrobe
The phrase 'building your wardrobe' doesn't refer to the actual creation of a wooden wardrobe from timber perfected by a carpenter and sold at an auction. It refers to what's inside of a wardrobe. The clothes you wear must have been intelligently

picked and accurately arranged. The following paragraphs will deal with how you should go about creating your own wardrobe and maintaining it.

Before we move further, let me just hold you back and reassure you that it is not against alpha male's principles to have a wardrobe. A wardrobe is not the sole property of female domination. An alpha male is not all about muscles and testicular hormones. An alpha male is judged by what he wears too.

Casual Occasion:

Your wardrobe should always contain at least five pairs of shorts, pyjamas and casual trousers, which can come handy for situations that are merely social or familial.

Official Occasions:

Your workplace must have official parties that you are required to attend. Basic common sense dictates that you cannot wear casual attire to such occasions. What you need is at least ten pairs of formal wears. Here is how you could pick the mentioned formals.

Go for a colour that is neither too bright nor too dull. An alpha male must always choose the midway, even when it comes to picking his clothes. A somber and mediocre colour always helps one leave a lasting impression on the onlookers in an official party. Parties that are sponsored and attended by workplaces are usually places where workers hope to impress higher officials and bosses. An alpha male is properly dressed could sway in his favour all the possible scales.

Social Occasions:

Social occasions could include anything ranging from a neighbors' day out in the garden to a gathering of long lost friends. If you seek to impress during such occasions, first try to measure the nature of the gathering. Is it too casual to wear something formal? Or is it too grave to go for casuals? Pick your clothes accordingly. As long as you do not feel out of place, you are good to go.

Accessories!

If your wardrobe were full of only clothing options, it would be nothing short of a fashion blunder for you. Make sure there are accessories options stacked sufficiently in your wardrobe. Make a little space, like a drawer for accommodating your accessories. Here is a little list of the regular accessories and the best ways to select them:

Ties

The impact a suitable tie has on onlookers is unimaginable. A tie might sound like such a small part of a man's personality but believe me the real game is played in between stripes and dots. You must brush up on your tie-selection technique if you wish to impress.

Stripped ties look good on shirts that are plain colored and do not follow a pattern of any kind. Similarly, dotted ties also rock a somber colored shirt. However, do not make the mistake of pairing up a plaid shirt and a striped or dotted tie. Such a combination is nothing short of a fashion faux pass. Plaid shirts are to be paired with plain colored ties while patterned shirts should go with designed or patterned ties. Remember this combination and you will never be embarrassed when it comes to ties.

Wrist Watch

What good is your forearm that you built so laboriously sweating it out for months in the gym, if it does not have a classy wrist watch to wear! Make sure that you always have a wristwatch on your arm, despite the nature of situation you are in.

Wearing a wristwatch on your arm says things about your personality. It denotes that you are a man who is organized and takes his time seriously. It implies that you do not indulge in follies that have no results or outcomes. A wristwatch on your left arm says more things about you than your entire wardrobe does.

The dial of your wristwatch could be either bigger or smaller than your arm width. However, most men look better when their wristwatch dials are smaller than their arm's width. The reason is pretty obvious; a forearm must look like one and a dial diminishes the quality of your forearm when it dominates it.

A metallic strap went out of fashion in the last decade. Unless properly carried, a metallic strapped wristwatch is a major turn off. Choose to go for leather straps instead of metallic. Leather straps are not only more comfortable but also look classier. Leather always compliments a man's personality.

Shoes

Women aren't the only ones that need to worry about getting their shoes right. A man's footwear conveys how classy he is. The right pair of shoes can make or break your entire impression on those around you. Be careful while choosing your shoes for the given occasion.

First off, make sure you polish whatever footwear you have. A dirty looking pair of footwear is as major a turn off as a potbelly. You do not want people to think that you do not pay attention to what you wear on your feet. Secondly, buy the proper equipment for taking care of your footwear. A cherry blossom, a brush of the right size and a used dirty cloth for cleaning inaccessible areas would do just fine for beginners. Lastly, buy a shoe rack if you do not have. When you allot your footwear a separate space to occupy, you make sure they are kept in an organized manner and that you can always make your selection by simply opening one door.

Black shoes are an evergreen choice. However, there are certain circumstances where you cannot simply afford to wear them. A casual gathering of friends or an outing with your colleagues does not require you to wear black footwear. For such occasions make sure you have stored in your shoe rack at least two pairs of casual footwear. This casual footwear could be a pair of light slippers or sports shoes. Again, know the occasion before selecting your shoes.

Socks

Do not be under the impression that what isn't visible isn't present. Your socks do matter, not as much as other accessories, but they do not have negligible value, either. Mismatched socks are not the way to go for someone seeking to be an alpha male. There are always such times in a day when you must take off your shoes to reveal what you are wearing beneath them.

Socks are also important because they decide half of the body odor you are supposed to carry. Most men smell from their feet. When you repeat your socks such an order intensifies and can go against you if it escapes your feet.

Nightwear

Though technically nightwear should fall under the category of clothes, but due its limited usage and specialty in regards of what they say about you, I have decided to include nightwear under 'accessories'.

Alan Anderson

Pay attention to what you wear to bed. Though there is no one to look during the mentioned duration, what you wear to bed has an everlasting impact on your personality. It ensures that you are always aware of your personality; that despite how tired or worn out you have become throughout the day, you have not forgotten to take care of your body. What you wear to bed is an indicator of how seriously you take your personality and to what lengths you are willing to go in order to maintain it. Lastly, being punctual about your nightwear shows that you are particular and slowly such an attitude is also ingrained into your mental faculties; so much so that it shows even during the day when you are not torn between boxers and undies.

As a candidate seeking the alpha male status, you should have a variety of options for nightwear. Boxers are a safe and wise choice since they are neither too short nor too long. They are of apt length and are sized enough to only suggest without appearing sleazy. Similarly, another good option is pyjamas. In some regions it is also known as a cardigan. Contrary to popular belief, a man in a pajama appears more trustworthy than one in a pair of undies. A pajama brings with itself the impression of domestication and stability. It says that the man wearing it is a man who could be blindly trusted. He would be a man worrying about housing loans and life insurances and not the upcoming weekend parties and the involved alcohol brands. There is something really erotic about pajamas that contribute towards the alpha male points scored by the man wearing them. Last but not the least; do not ignore your undies. What you wear beneath your pants has as much impact as what you wear above them. Go for brands that are known and reputed instead of locally made undies which could be badly designed and the threads from such products could create issues like rashes and other problems. Wear the right size. If your package is heavy, look for undies that have a bigger much in the front. Likewise, a small package should go with normal sized underwear.

Clothes are your resumes. What you show is what is bought at the start. Impressions built at the initial stages work wonders for you. Pay ample attention to your wardrobe since a man is known more by what he wears than by anything else. Having or maintaining a wardrobe is not the sole dominion of females. When you are in the habit of maintaining a wardrobe, you get to develop necessary habits like punctuality, particularity, and discipline- traits considered highly valuable in an alpha male.

Physique

If there is any single thing that comes to one's mind when the word 'manliness' is uttered, it's a masculine body with ripped arms and toned muscles all over it. Regardless of your sex, a toned body is always appreciated in any walk of life. It is not just a health requirement but has increasingly become a trend to be followed. The more muscled a man is, the better man he is presumed to be. An alpha male must always pay attention to how tone his body is at all times. For the same purpose, the following steps have been recommended:

Join the nearby gym with the provision of a personal trainer. Inquire about a well-equipped gym in your area and ask for personal trainers for you.

Since you will be a beginner, do not stress too much on getting a ripped body and instead focus on either gaining fat or losing it, depending upon whether you are overweight or underweight.

Make sure your diet is compatible with your gym goals. Include a lot of protein in your diet and avoid consumption of oily and spicy food. Quit eating out and especially ordering junk food from joints. You need to make sure that what you eat is nothing short of a balanced diet. A balanced diet is nothing but the right amount of each food present in the right proportion in your meal. A balanced diet provides all the necessary nutrients and minerals to your body thereby enriching it with everything it wants.

The basic requirement of a good physique is that it must be fed and made healthy first. You cannot hope to get a gym-toned body from day one itself. You need to exercise patience while building a body. The process takes time and the resultant body cannot be achieved overnight.

Prepare a list of objectives that you would like to attain before subscribing to a heavy gymming plan. Take it day by day or week by week. Your objectives must be in sync with your ability and time. Do not have unrealistic goals set for yourself in the gym.

You must always push yourself to reach better results and a more toned body. It is only by constantly pushing and expanding your limits that you can grow. However, you must also guard against overdoing it. Building a body is important to achieve the alpha male status but there is nothing more important than your well-being.

Categorize your gym training into specific parts and you will realize that such categorization works wonders for you. Allot each day of the week specific areas of your body to work on. Take it step by step instead of rushing it all together.

Make a schedule of your entire week and try to fit in the gymming time in it. Do not just pick up your shorts and go gymming whenever you find the time to. Make sure you follow a strict timetable to gym, so that you also learn the art of discipline on the go.

A ripped body is the ultimate dream of every guy and the ultimate fantasy of every chick. Barring exceptions, it's a healthy and toned up body that attracts people towards each other romantically. The romantic quotient not just enhances the appeal of an alpha male but also increases his chances of getting some action.

An alpha male does not simply build a body. He takes care of it on a daily basis. He may not go to a gym at a particular time every day, but he takes some time out to jog, push up or do some work which keeps him in shape. He makes sure that he is not just fit but healthy.

A masculine body is more than just a treat to the eyes. A man who bothers enough to build a good physique sends out a really positive message. A man who spends time in the gym is taken to be patient and passionate. When the t-shirt fits perfectly into your arms, there is a definite surge in your self-confidence and you no longer suffer from body issues. It implies that he knows how to take care of whatever he is bestowed with. It shows that he is a man who likes to perfect things and does a lot of handwork to achieve the same. A man who works out is a man you can probably trust. He would be the one having your back in unfortunate situations. When a man develops a ripped physique he inspires faith and awe. If you seek to become the next alpha, wake up from your sleep, quit the beanbag and start working out. You may not end up with a good body within a month but hang in there, little buddy. However, it needs to be mentioned here that a muscled body is not everything that an alpha male has. He could be a sorry cut figure of a fragile human being and yet be the alpha male of the group. But a good physique always adds a good advantage to your resume as an alpha male.

Chapter 7 – Alpha Male And His Tongue

Welcome to the seventh chapter of this book. Despite how dirty the title of this chapter sounds, I assure you it is not what you think it is. This chapter has been specially designed to walk you through an ideal alpha male and his tongue-behaviour, which is to say what he speaks.

In the previous chapter, we saw how an alpha male must take care to make sure his wardrobe is not just updated but also apt. We learnt about the necessary ingredients of an ideal alpha male wardrobe. We got to know that what you wear is as important as anything else. However, this chapter is the polar opposite of the previous one. Here we are to learn about the ideal speaking behaviour of an alpha male. After all, you are what you say, they say.

If there is one weapon in the world that can outsmart even the nuclear missiles from Russia, it's words. Words have the inexhaustible energy to not just create wonders but also to destroy empires. They have the capacity to make and break you. Mince your words and you could be losing out on a multimillion-dollar deal. On the other hand, get them right and you stand to win the game of thrones. The power words hold cannot be simply put to words. They can alter the fate of civilizations and decide the course of history. Like I said at the start, they are the ultimate weapons.

How is this chapter relevant to the context this book has been written in? Words and masculinity; they both do not seem to fit, do they? Let us discover.

The alpha male in the group can always be distinguished from a distance. You do not have to announce their arrival since their mere presence would do it in a way. The alpha male would never speak when it is not warranted for him to. He would keep his mouth shut until the right time to speak. When he speaks, everyone listens.

Your personality of that of an alpha male is dictated by a numerous amount of factors. Looks, charisma, body postures, decision-making capabilities; the list goes on longer and higher than the Great Wall of China. But one of the important factors that most people miss out on while addressing ways to achieve an alpha male personality is speaking.

What You Speak

An alpha male rarely minces his words. He knows the exact contents of his speaking. He knows better than to simply go on a verbal diarrhea and swing words as he goes. He is a prepared orator, one who knows what his ingredients are, their advantages, shortcomings and possible suggestions.

An alpha male does not invent words on the spot, nor does he 'think of' something when the right times comes. When it comes to speaking, an alpha male is either always prepared or comes with his homework done. If you aspire to be an alpha male, you must first learn your research skills. Imagine having to talk to a crowd, for the purpose of convincing them of your beliefs. Do you randomly walk up to the stage, grab the mike and start blabbering whatever comes to your mind? Or do you go home, do your homework, make a list of the points you will be touching, come back and start dressing the crowd in a dignified manner? It is obvious that as a seeker of alpha male status you will go for the latter and naturally so because a speech that is unprepared and under researched is bound to affect your impressions.

The contents of your speech are a vital factor in deciding your alpha male status. An alpha male speaks only those things that are absolutely necessary without much fussing. An alpha male is eloquent and knows his 'their' from 'there'. He knows how to keep it short, informative and yet inclusive.

How You Speak

Naturally the most vital factor of speech, the manner of your speech is more important than its contents. It's how you speak that matters more than that what you speak.

An ideal alpha male knows the apt manner of speaking when it comes to situations that demand a specific style. He knows how to address crowds, unions and masses. He knows how to talk in front of a help seeker. He knows the consoling words for a griever. He is aware of the tone modulations one must do according to varying conditions. Moods and their respective tones are all registered in the alpha male's mind directory and he can command them at will.

Gentle

An alpha male is gentle in speech for certain situations. Such situations could be a woman asking for help or a downtrodden member of the group seeking advice and consolation. An alpha male is supposed to be the father figure of the group and such a personality needs to be caring and affectionate. Love and care can be displayed with the usage of the right words, and more often than not, it is the gentle words that do the trick.

Soft

The difference between being gentle and being soft is that when you are being gentle you are being so in terms of your behaviour while when you are being soft, you are being so with regards to your tone and voice-volume. An alpha male is not just gentle but also soft. You need to not only regulate how loud you speak but also how frequently you do it also.

Firm

Just because an alpha male is supposed to be a people-pleaser and hence should be gentle and soft in speech does not mean he cannot be firm while being the previous two. Being firm in speech is all about being honest, straight and unwavering while you speak.

Firmness in speech need not be pointed out or displayed separately. The way you speak automatically shows that you are resolute on your points and have done sufficient research to not sway from them. Your stand is yours and no one else's.

When You Speak

An alpha male knows knottiest what and how to speak but also WHEN to speak. There is a time for every tiniest thing on this planet. Your wall clock never shows a proper time. You need to calculate it by experience and common sense. An alpha male does not start blabbering the first opportunity he gets at throwing his views on people's faces.

An alpha male knows when to shut his gob and when to offer his opinions. The timing of an opinion is as important as its contents. You may have a rich vocabulary and a gruff old baritone to boast of, but if you are a speaker who has no idea regarding when to open his mouth and when to shut it, you are as good as a mute.

The timing of your speaking must not only be perfect but also appropriate. You should know when your view is required and when it is not. Not only should you pay attention to such times but also keep a track of how such situations arise. There is always a pattern coming out in a conversation, which may help you predict the exact time when your view could be of importance to the crowd. It is only when you are able to finally learn how to calculate or anticipate such times that you evolve as a speaker. There are times when no one wants your opinion. There are times when no one wants your opinion but it is essential for the greater good that you put forth it in front of everyone regardless of whether someone wishes it or not. Then there are times when everyone requires you to speak. Learn the art of gauging the situation and classifying it under the given heads. Always look for chances when someone has made a mistake. Grab the opportunity with both the hands and speak. There is no such thing as the right time to speak. Like it has been mentioned at the start of this chapter, no clock in the world has its dial programmed to tell you the correct time when you should speak. It is only with experience in group conversations and a certain amount of common sense that you will be able to learn estimating the time when you must speak.

No Bullshit Attitude

An alpha male never beats around the bush. If asked to speak on a topic, he would quickly cut to the chase and speak only those points that he thinks is relevant to the crowd, topics discussion and time constrains. He would not waste your time in going into the history of the given topic, it is possible impact in the future or the various expectations people have out of it. He will tell you hardcore facts that have been proven and will help you save your time.

Did you attend or participate in debates when you were in school? Or maybe wrote essays on environments and world peace in standard eighth? If yes, you would know what I am about to explain. Bullshit speaking is an action that is done to not just evade the central point that is completely avoided but also to mislead the conversation towards a direction entirely irrelevant and disconnected to the topic of conversation.

Alan Anderson

When an alpha male speaks, people listen. He stands out among the crowd because he is straight and comes across as an honest person. If you wish to become an alpha male in terms of speech, you must learn the art of trimming everything that is unnecessary that including all that is desirable and relevant. Know how to differentiate between the mundane and the important. It becomes evident from an alpha male's speaking that he is a man who has experience, research and gravity in whatever he is speaking about. No one sees him as someone who is winging it at the go or speaking out of his backside.

The art of speaking is vital to the establishment of an alpha male status. An alpha male knows what, how, when and how much to speak. He rarely deviates from the point and believes in keeping it to the point and as true as possible. He is suave, gentle, polite and richly gifted in the vocabulary department. His choice of words is classy, simple and yet rich. He could hold an audience captivated without letting them move away from the topic at hand even for a single moment. His crowd is not bored for even the tiniest fragment of a second and understands him as he speaks. An alpha male knows how to capture his audience. He uses the simplest of words to lead you into a story. An alpha male is a great storyteller. He would gather his life experiences in a bundle and take out one by one according to the situation and context. He has his own share of tales to tell. His audience is not just smitten with him but also adore him for his speaking abilities.

An alpha male is the complete orator. He knows everything there is to know about public speaking. He is aware about the importance of the exact time to pause, hold a breath and even the occasional sighing. You can always find prototypes of an ideal alpha male addressing a crowd at a social gathering, or motivating a group of youngsters in a rally or even leading a protest march against an unjustified government ban. The examples of alpha males being good orators are aplenty in our world. However, it is necessary to note that the reverse is not impliedly true. Not all good orators are necessarily cut out for becoming alpha males. They may have the gift of the gab but when it comes to fulfilling the rest of the requirements of an ideal alpha male, they fall short of the standards so asked. The art of speaking is just one part of the entire ideal alpha male personality. It adds to the appeal of an alpha male and doesn't form the whole package. Despite that, it is an essential feather to be collected for your hat.

The alpha male has the capacity to pull off unimaginable feats by words alone. He is the man who has mastered ways to derive the maximum output from the application of the right words. In order to do so, he must first have a rich vocabulary. If you wish to develop your vocabulary, start with reading the morning newspaper. Find out meanings of all the words you did not understand by referring to the Internet or a dictionary. These days, they are letting you download offline dictionaries on your smartphones. A good vocabulary always gets you the brownie points. An alpha male makes full use of a brimming vocabulary to leave behind good impressions. An alpha male knows the right word selection according to the appropriate situation.

You will never find an alpha male fumbling with his words. He takes his time, pauses in between, broods over words and lets them out in a proper fashion. His tone, style and manner are all well suited to the circumstance he is speaking in. It hence, goes without saying that an alpha male is an excellent orator. He has the charm to hold audience for hours.

You can tell a lot about a person from the way they speak. What you speak eventually becomes your identity. A good example of this is inspirational quotes left to us by great people. A mere look at the brilliantness of some of the truly inspirational quotes by Mahatma Gandhi and Plato and other such notable figures and you could describe their character. In a similar fashion, an alpha male is also judged on the basis of what and how he speaks. Every word that comes out of his mouth gets counted and weighed. If you wish to become an alpha male and are working on your speech department, here is a brief list of suggestions for you. Speak only that is important; trim the irrelevant parts. Speak less in the given time. Do not consume too much time of your audience. Stick to a format and do not bore your audience with facts and figures. Try to include anecdotes and funny examples to add a bit of humour. Try to maintain eye contact with your audience. The more eye contacts you made, the more honest you come across as a speaker. Fumbling is okay; remember that; but correcting it is the key. Practice before a mirror an hour before you are about to make your speech. Fumbling could be kept in check that way. Another thing that needs be kept in mind is that you must rich your vocabulary whenever it is possible. A good vocabulary is a sexy thing to be a proud owner of and it never hurts to present good words while speaking.

Chapter 8 – Basic Features Of An Alpha Male That You Must Incorporate Into Your Personality

Welcome to the eighth chapter of this e-book. This chapter has been specially designed to make you aware of the basic characteristic features of an alpha male that you need to incorporate into your lives so as to move some steps further in the direction of becoming one. Keep in mind that this chapter does not guarantee you overnight transition into a walking talking mass of masculine oomph but can only promise to show you the way. I believe it is time we moved forward without much ado.

The following paragraphs will contain some very basic properties of an average alpha male that may help you in your journey towards ultimate masculinity.

Responsible

An alpha male is a responsible person. He knows what is expected of him and goes about doing his work accordingly. The trait of being responsible is a rare trait and cannot be expected to be present in herd people.

The difference between common folk and an alpha male is that the former category people do not feel burdened under an expectation. These are the kind of people who follow the entire herd and do not consider themselves to be responsible for anything major happening to the group. The latter category, which is the alpha males, on the other hand, are mature people who know their tasks well and act according to them. An alpha male would never ignore his responsibilities and always make them his first priority. He would find out ways to deal with problems arising out of him not being able to fulfill his responsibilities. He would be prepared for the worst case scenario and do a mental drilling of all that could happen if things went wrong.

Only the leader of the group can be expected to bear responsibilities like a true man. Such an expectation has been always present in the human race. In pre historic times, every tribe would have a leader who would make key decisions and give out orders. Cut to the present day and you will find a leader and subsequent team leaders in every corporate set up. Such people are alpha males in their own way since they are responsible for their entire group. If the team suffers a defeat, it will be them who will take the blame. If the team comes out with flying colours, a major part of the appreciation will be naturally saved for them.

A Complete Leader

An alpha male is a natural leader. Every group has a captain, a leader, a monitor and a boss. A leader has different names for different places, times and situations. However way you spell or call it, whoever is responsible for the success of a group and takes care of everything and everyone in it is a leader of the group.

Leader vs. Boss

An alpha male, in order to be so, must be a leader. Leadership is not synonymous to bossing though. The difference between a leader and a boss is that a boss would direct people to work while a leader would get down his high pedestrian and work alongside his people. A leader is a people's person and not just a fat king sitting the throne and ordering around the castle. A leader knows his people and their capabilities and shortcomings.

An alpha male not only knows his people but also interacts with them on a regular basis. He is familiar with the traits of his group's members. He is the only person in the entire group who knows the best way to start using these traits for the greater good of the team. These traits are like sleeping volcanoes; they will not be activated unless pushed to do so. A leader recognizes the true potential of all such people and pushes them to perform at their peaks. A leader knows the limitations and peaking speed of his group's members and is aware of the right amount of inspiration required to ignite such traits to fruition.

The difference between a leader and a boss is the difference between Hitler and Gandhi. Both led a nation but while Hitler gave orders from high up his horse, Gandhi decided to work with his people rather than sitting in comfort and shouting orders from atop his throne.

An alpha male is not a boss but a leader. He knows his team inside out. He knows the limits he can push his group to. He is familiar with individual capacities and how each individual can be allowed a particular role. If a member is having a bad day, he can feel confident about talking it out with the leader just as if he is no one but a close friend. The impression a leader leaves on his group is warm and really comfortable. A leader is not someone whom everyone fears but he is rather someone everyone respects. Being a leader is synonymous to being able to inspire respect and awe. It does not need to be announced that the leader has arrived in the room. When a leader enters the room, everyone is suddenly aware of his presence simply by the way he walks. He is the sole person in the room who does not need an introduction of any kind. He is aware of each and every member of his group and is in personal touch with them.

A great leader pushes you to your extremes. However, a boss doesn't care about you or your capabilities. Your boss may not even be aware of your personal and individual abilities. However, if you are under a leader, he is familiar with what you can do and what you cannot. A leader brings out the best in you by stretching you to your worst. He is ready to pull you back in the moment you start breaking; however till you do, he won't refrain from exposing to your worst fears. He will encourage you to break all your previous records of achievement. He won't let you rest until you complete your race. He will shout at you, swear at you and even console you when you breakdown but he won't give up on you. Such a person will stand by you no matter what. He will be your father figure by your thick and thin. No matter how bad you screw up your game, he will come to your side and hold you. He will not fight your battles but will push you to do so, on your own. Such a man is the ideal person to have in your life as you will have a constant support and guiding light.

An alpha male's personality is not very different from that of a leader. The traits of a leader and an alpha male aren't very distinctive in nature. When you look close enough, you will realize that a man who is a natural born leader is highly likely to turn himself into a man who has high chances of becoming an alpha male.

Decision Making

Whatever group it may be, whichever end result it may be working towards and however charismatic leader it may be led by, if the decisions that are being taken in the group are haywire and not efficient, there is something wrong with the alpha male of the team.

Being able to decide right from wrong, left from right, white from black and this from that is a rare quality. Many people are unable to differentiate between such simple things in life that are, to add to the shock, stark contrasts of each other. The ability to decide and choose is an important trait that should be present in large amounts with anyone who has been accorded the title of an alpha male.

An alpha male as we studied a page ago, is a responsible man. Upon his shoulders rest the entire see saw of victory and defeat. He will be held responsible for anything the team goes through, achieves and fails in. In such a scenario, it is vital that the alpha male makes all the right decisions with wisdom, agility and prudence.

Prudence is that quality of a person that keeps his reasonable in his approach to anything in life. In other words it can be said that the quality of prudence is an important part of an alpha male personality. A prudent person is a reasonable person and takes calls based on classic logic.

Wisdom is a primary ingredient in the dish called 'decision'. Wisdom is not gained overnight. No book in the world can teach you how to achieve wisdom unless you have suffered enough to know it. Wisdom is not knowledge. Knowledge is what you know; wisdom is the acceptance that you don't. You may be thirsty for knowledge but you will never be thirsty for wisdom. Wisdom humbles you; knowledge makes you proud. Knowledge can be gained from books and scripts but wisdom comes with experience and a good amount of common sense. An alpha male is wise and makes informed decisions.

It is not always possible to keep a cool head as there's clamoring going on around you. Imagine being expected to make a crucial decision at such a time of peril. Not only are you likely to go with the wrong choice, but you are also likely to choose an option that might backfire on your entire team. An alpha male is capable of keeping his head cool while making all the difficult choices.

Choices are tough to make when they are made for others. An alpha male does exactly that. He is responsible for what happens to the team after he presses the enter button. Hence it becomes extremely important that an alpha male makes good decisions in the right time.

Recognizes Potential

A team or a group is not all about its head. Clearly, all the members in a group are individually as important as the leader. However, due to his position being an administratively important one, the leader does get to make calls on important and vital matters, without diminishing the value of the rest of the members.

Each member of the group has some sort of potential that can be used for the betterment of the group in the journey towards achievement of some goal. An alpha male knows how best to tap into this potential of a member and how best to use it for the mentioned purpose. An alpha male spends considerable amount of time visiting his camp, inquiring around his personnel and updating himself regarding each and every member's condition. When he does such an exercise, he gets to know many things. Out of these things some of the most important ones are - a member's skills, restrictions, inhibitions and areas for improvement. He makes a mental map of all the individuals he met, talked to and listened to during his visits and enlists them there. He is now equipped to call anyone to test and try them. After this assessment stage is complete, the alpha male now allots each member the work he thinks is fit for them according to the inferences drawn from his assessment.

An alpha leader must always be on the lookout for talent and good skills. Having an eye open for possible candidates always helps not just him but also the team. Having known his team inside out, he is at a good position to assign work and expect results.

Accountability

The alpha male is a man burdened with responsibilities. There are two scenarios in which the alpha male is held responsible: when the team achieves success and when it faces a defeat. In both the situations it is the alpha male who is held responsible for the outcome. Being the caption of the squad it is the alpha male's duty to ensure that whatever decision he is taking is in the team's best interest and propels it towards a win.

However, the best breed of alpha male does something different when it comes to accountability. This breed stands up and takes all the blame when the team under-performs or fails. He goes into damage control mode and tries to minimize the effect of the recent loss. However when the team wins, a true alpha male steps down and lets the entire team take credit of it, thereby diluting the value of his role in the win, despite how large it may have been. An alpha male is all for accountability, but as soon as the credits start pouring in; he folds his hands and stands in the corner so as to allow his group to bask in the glory.

Charismatic

Though not the strictest of requirements, a charismatic leader who seeks to be the alpha male of the group is always a good thing. After having put in all your efforts into becoming the ultimate masculine presence in your group, if you sprinkle a little charisma over the top, the dish becomes unbeatable.

No one is able to resist charisma being oozed out from a man who is responsible, leader and a decision maker. When you are charismatic, people not just look up to you but also look AT you. Charisma in a potential alpha male is a crowd puller and can surely get the ladies in your favour. Though it sounds shallow to gain attention by something that relies on looks, but you got to do what you got to do. Charisma provides that initial push that most leaders lack. When you are charismatic, you naturally become the hot topic of discussion and are favored over anyone who has arrived having switched off his charm button. Charisma is not a trait to really boast about, however, it can tilt the scales in your favor. Charisma is not synonymous to good looks though. You could be charismatic when you do not look very attractive. It is more about how you come across as rather than how you look. It is also about how you carry your own self, despite whatever you are wearing or however you are looking. Turn on that charisma button to unleash the alpha male inside of you.

Creative

An alpha male is not all about muscles and good decisions. On a personal level, an alpha male is a highly developed person. To top all his skills, an alpha male is a creative personality. He does not believe in following the crowd. There has got to be something special about a person who inspires so many people.

Creativity is a rare trait. Painters, poets and authors are usually the people who are blessed with a knack for innovation. A person is said to be creative when he has a tendency to do the same thing as others but in a different way. Again, creativity is said to have been used when a particular result is achieved through an innovative way that distinguishes itself from the normal methods. Being creative is about standing out of the crowd. It is about outshining all your competition because you have got that creative edge. An alpha male is a creative person.

Non-creative people are stagnant in their lives. An alpha male cannot afford to remain at one stage. His job is to keep the momentum going and the wheels turning. In order to achieve the same he must make sure that his group does not become a pool of still water. He must ensure that his group is a running stream instead. Being a creative person, an alpha male knows the ways in which he can not only increase the productivity of the group but also involve maximum participation while ensuring enjoyment in the process.

Why Is Creativity So Important A Trait For An Alpha Male?

The quality of being creative makes all the difference in this world of cutthroat competition. There are numerous entities, be it groups or individuals, that are sitting ready to challenge you at the forte you claim you are a genius at. When you happen to be the alpha male of your group, there is an extra burden on your head to make sure your group is always prepared for a standoff.

Creativity gives your group an apprehension when it comes to such stand offs.

A creative man is a man open to all kinds of possibilities. This man would not say no tottering something out of the ordinary. He would give the green flag to innovative and eccentric ideas and encourage young minds to come up with their own suggestions for improving and enhancing the performance of the group.

The trait of creativity suggests that the human mind is as important as the human muscle. It denotes that what you think and how you think are equally important factors for determination of your alpha male status as any other qualities that you might possess. When you are creative, you automatically open your mind to a numerous amount of trial and errors. By allowing yourself these chances of mistakes, you are letting yourself learn. It is only by failing that one learns. One who always wins learns nothing.

A group has regular competition from other groups. That is how it has always been. Right from the days of the dawn of our planet earth, man has always competed. Struggling to survive by eliminating competition has always been in our gene pool. However, every group is almost at the same level of competence as others. The amount of competition has increased so much that there is not much difference left between two randomly picked competitors. The technical know-how, talents and technology are all the same for everyone. How does one then ensure one's win? Creativity is the answer. An alpha male who is creative enough to pave the way of victory for his group is a true leader. Opening up to new avenues and horizons is not sufficient. The alpha leader should also be willing to do all it takes to implement his creativity in effective practical terms.

Tolerance

Such a competitive world rarely allows us to pause and catch our breaths. It is important that we not just survive the race but also not break down under the stress it subjects us to. An alpha male makes sure that the group survives such a race and does not falter in doing so.

On a personal front, an alpha male is a man who has great levels of tolerance. He is a calm, composed and patient man who has all the time in the world to listen to even the least productive person in the entire system. He would always be more than happy to sit down, share a cup of coffee and listen to your woes despite how busy his schedule is. An alpha male has the power to tolerate not just the stress of handling the team but also the burden of leading the team to success. An ideal alpha male never snaps and is rarely seen frowning at someone for bad performance. An alpha leader first calls the person badly performing to him, has a nice little talk and encourages him to do better. You could never witness an alpha male getting pissed at his subordinates for petty reasons. A true alpha would never give an earful to a person in front of his colleagues. He would choose to do it in private. However, if it is a genuine alpha leader you are dealing with, and you have been called for an earful, it is certain that you must have done something really bad, or enhanced the frequency of your bad performance. However, a very brilliant thing about alpha leaders is that they give you second chances to right your wrongs.

A stern face, a composed stature, a straight back and a poker face or one with a smile on it; alpha males are the ultimate epitome of patience. They are not egoistic or introverts. They would tell you where you are wrong without offending you. Their levels of endurance are really high and you can rely on them to sail the ship to calm waters.

Chapter 9 – Masculinity: A Changing Concept

Welcome to the ninth and the final chapter of this e-book. We shall deal with the ever-changing concept of what makes a man a man here. Let us challenge the staunch idea of masculinity and check whether it can wax and wane or not.

An alpha male is the supreme leader of the pack. He is a man assumed to possess extreme masculine features like a good physique, endurance and toughness. These standard forms of masculinity have undergone major changes in the last few decades. The idea of an alpha male has eventually transformed majorly through times.

In the traditional sense of the word, masculinity does not permit something as lighthearted as **Humour**. However, an alpha male is supposed to be a humorous man. He is the storyteller of the group, the anecdote-giver and the experience sharer. Humour is essential for life and sometimes mandatory.

For a group to stick together, occasional dosages of humour is desirable. An alpha male knows not just how to make fun but also how to be the subject of jokes himself. He knows how to take jokes in his stride and not take them seriously.

An alpha male is a flexible man as opposed to the rigid prototype he is assumed to be. Flexibility is a good feather in an alpha male's cap as he can learn to adapt to different and changing circumstances and does not become stagnant.

Flexibility is what sets the alpha male apart from other ordinary leaders. An alpha male knows when to bend the knee and when to pick the sword. The alpha male is wise enough to know when to speak and when to listen.

Endurance is the quality of sustaining and surviving. It is that trait that lets you retain yourself in a fierce competition. The odds may be stacked against you, lady luck may not be in your side and you may be having a bad day but despite all that if you manage to at least survive the race, you are said to be enduring. An alpha male has his endurance levels really high.

Tact is something the traditional alpha male lacked. A few decades ago, an alpha male could never be imagined to possess the trait of tact. Tact is knowing what, when and how to manipulate, speak and act so as to settle for the best possible option for you. If not for tact, the world would have been in shambles today. An alpha male knows the best tactical ways to get results for his group.

The quality to **evolve** is golden. The ability to evolve yourself speaks a lot about your personality and frame of mind. Evolution is not child's play. It takes a lot of effort to be able to transform into a new self. Evolution implies that you have left your old self behind and are ready to embrace some changes in your life. An alpha male is always ready to evolve.

Learning is what keeps us going. It could be in any field. There is no such thing as 'enough learning'. The sea of knowledge is gigantic and no man has drunk all of it and lived. An alpha male is always eager to learn. This curiosity to learn propels him towards things undiscovered and unearthed. He not only gets to know about stuff he didn't know before but also realizes the vastness of it all.

As opposed to the traditional prototype, an alpha male would prefer ruling over learning, our new generation alpha male is not such a close- minded guy. He would prefer learning even from the most humble of sources. For an alpha male, there need not be a classroom and professor in order for them to learn. Learning for them is a constant process that keeps running inside their minds.

The bottom-line of this chapter is that the image of a typical alpha male is fast changing and rightly so because as opposed to a rigid and unwavering standard alpha male in the past, the new version is more realistic, practical and feasible.

Conclusion

Thank you again for downloading this book!

I hope this book was able to help you develop the skills and confidence you need to attract the women you want, be on top of your chosen professional career, earn the respect and admiration of your peers, and in general imbibe what it takes to become an alpha male.

The next step is to integrate the positive insights you have learned from this book into your day-to-day activities. As has been sufficiently underscored in this book, becoming an alpha male is not an overnight endeavor. It takes time and a degree of consistency to bring to life the changes you want to take effect in your life.

As such, regardless of the challenges you come across, you should not let up in your desire to be the best and to stand out among the rest of your peers. Know that being an alpha male is not merely a choice you make, but a lifestyle you need to remain committed to over the long haul.

Finally, I'd like to ask you a favor if I may. If you enjoyed this book, then I'd really appreciate you leaving a review and your feedback on Amazon.

Thank you and good luck!

Alan Anderson